I0013520

The AI-Powered IDE Cursor Explained

A Practical Guide to Automating and Enhancing Your Coding Workflow

MILA ASHFORD

TABLE OF CONTENTS

Introduction

The world of software development is changing—again. But this time, it's not just another framework or language update. It's a shift so profound that it's redefining what it means to write code. At the heart of this evolution is something more intuitive than syntax, more powerful than a debugger, and more human than we ever imagined—artificial intelligence. And leading this revolution, quietly but confidently, is a tool that's turning heads and transforming workflows: Cursor.

Imagine an IDE that doesn't just wait for your instructions, but thinks alongside you. One that reads between the lines of your code, anticipates your needs, and offers suggestions that feel like second nature. Cursor isn't just another coding assistant, it's the first true AI-powered development partner. Whether you're fixing bugs, refactoring legacy code, building something new from scratch, or collaborating on complex projects, Cursor meets you at your level and then gently pushes you higher.

But let's get real. With every new tool comes a wave of hype, tutorials, and promises of productivity that often don't match reality. That's why this book exists—not to echo the buzz, but to cut through it. Whether you're a beginner looking for your footing in the world of AI-enhanced programming or an experienced developer seeking deeper control and customization, this guide walks with you. It's not just about showing you what Cursor can do, it's about helping you unlock your own creative power through it.

We're not here to marvel at technology for its own sake. We're here to understand it, master it, and make it work for us. Cursor isn't just changing how we code, it's changing how we *think* about code. And once you experience the seamless dance between human logic and machine intelligence, you'll never want to go back.

So open your mind, fire up your curiosity, and get ready to discover a new way of building software. Because the next generation of developers won't just write code—they'll collaborate with it. And this, right here, is your invitation to the future.

Chapter 1

The Rise of AI in Development Environments

The Evolution of Integrated Development Environments (IDEs)

The journey of software development has always mirrored the pace of technological advancement. In the earliest days, developers relied on basic text editors and command-line interfaces to write, compile, and debug code. This process was cumbersome and highly manual, demanding an in-depth understanding of syntax, compilation steps, and external debugging tools. Yet, from those modest beginnings, the concept of an Integrated Development Environment (IDE) was born—a single application that unified multiple tools to streamline the entire coding lifecycle.

In the 1980s and 1990s, IDEs like Turbo Pascal and Borland C++ revolutionized how developers interacted with code. These environments brought together a code editor, compiler, and debugger in one place. Suddenly, programmers could write, compile, and test code in a seamless loop. As graphical user interfaces became more powerful, modern IDEs such as Eclipse, NetBeans, and Microsoft Visual Studio emerged, bringing with them advanced features like real-time error highlighting, code completion, syntax checking, and project management capabilities.

With the rise of open-source platforms and the explosive growth of web development, newer IDEs like JetBrains' IntelliJ IDEA, Atom, and Visual Studio Code reshaped expectations again. These tools provided modularity, rich plugin ecosystems, and deep language integrations. VS Code, in particular, became a community favorite for its speed, customizability, and robust support for multiple languages and frameworks.

Despite all this progress, even the most feature-rich IDEs were fundamentally reactive. They waited for input, validated code, and offered static suggestions based on preconfigured rules. There was intelligence, yes—but not intuition. These environments enhanced productivity but didn't fundamentally change the cognitive workflow of software engineering. Developers still had to drive the entire process manually: planning, thinking through logic, searching for patterns, debugging, and optimizing. And this is where the next seismic shift was brewing.

The Role of Artificial Intelligence in Coding Tools

The integration of artificial intelligence into software development tools wasn't an overnight phenomenon. Early signs appeared in the form of smarter autocomplete engines—tools like IntelliSense and predictive typing systems that analyzed static code context to offer suggestions. But the real breakthrough came with the emergence of large language models (LLMs), trained on a vast corpora of code and natural language, capable of understanding programming logic, context, and intent.

At its core, AI in development is about context awareness. Traditional IDEs might recognize a function definition and suggest parameters, but AI models can infer what you're trying to build and offer relevant solutions—even generating blocks of code from plain English prompts. They can spot potential bugs, recommend optimizations, or even explain unfamiliar code in simple terms. This is not just automation; it's augmentation.

The rise of tools like GitHub Copilot, powered by OpenAI's Codex model, demonstrated just how transformative this technology could be. Developers could write comments in natural language, and AI would generate corresponding code. Entire functions could be scaffolded within seconds. It wasn't perfect, but it was undeniably powerful. And it sparked a wave of AI-first coding assistants, each seeking to push the boundaries of what was possible.

What makes AI truly disruptive in this space is its ability to learn and adapt. AI tools aren't bound by rigid rules—they're probabilistic, capable of handling ambiguity and generating creative solutions. As models grew more sophisticated, they began handling more complex tasks: writing unit tests, identifying security flaws, and even participating in architectural discussions. It blurred the line between developer and assistant, between tool and teammate.

However, most of these AI-infused tools were bolted onto existing IDEs as plugins or extensions. They improved the coding experience but remained somewhat disjointed—still requiring manual oversight, lacking deep integration, and often feeling like external agents rather than integral components of the developer's workspace. The development community was still waiting for something more native, seamless, and contextually aware. Enter Cursor AI.

How Cursor AI Stands Out in the AI Coding Landscape

Cursor AI isn't just another extension or plugin; it's a full-fledged IDE designed from the ground up with AI at its core. It reimagines the development experience by making artificial intelligence not an accessory but a co-pilot deeply embedded within every part of the workflow. It doesn't simply assist—it collaborates.

What distinguishes Cursor from other AI-powered tools is its native, proactive intelligence. Rather than merely offering suggestions when prompted, Cursor actively monitors your coding process, understands your intent, and dynamically adjusts its behavior. It engages in real-time conversations about your code, asks clarifying questions, and offers well-structured solutions. This is pair programming at its most evolved—with an assistant who not only knows how to write code but understands *why* you're writing it.

Cursor is built on the powerful OpenAI Codex and GPT models, but it also introduces a unique agent-based system that tracks project-wide context. It understands your file structure, dependencies, naming conventions, and even your coding style. This allows it to produce more accurate and maintainable code. Rather than just generating generic boilerplate, it crafts solutions that fit seamlessly into your existing codebase.

Moreover, Cursor goes beyond coding. It can write documentation, generate README files, produce comprehensive commit messages, and help manage version control. It can explain complex logic, refactor legacy code, and even detect architectural inconsistencies. The IDE isn't just a tool for output—it's an environment for dialogue between human creativity and machine precision.

Another standout feature is Cursor's emphasis on **local tooling with AI augmentation**. While many AI tools rely heavily on the cloud for everything, Cursor strikes a balance. It leverages local processing for speed and privacy while using the power of the cloud when necessary. This hybrid approach means developers can trust Cursor to be fast, secure, and scalable, especially for team and enterprise use.

Cursor is also built with collaboration in mind. Multiple developers can engage with the same AI assistant in a shared environment, creating a unified development experience across teams. This collaborative intelligence allows for more coherent codebases, fewer integration issues, and a faster development cycle.

Where Cursor really shines, though, is in its **intuitive user experience**. The interface is clean, modern, and minimal. Yet behind its simplicity lies a powerful engine capable of understanding not just code syntax but developer intention. You don't have to be an AI expert to use Cursor. Its design ensures that whether you're a junior developer just learning to write loops or a senior engineer building distributed systems, you get value immediately.

In a market flooded with tools that promise productivity, Cursor delivers transformation. It redefines what an IDE can be—not just a space to write code, but a living, thinking workspace where ideas evolve, errors are caught in real time, and creative solutions emerge through interaction.

This is the beginning of a new paradigm in software development—where humans and machines collaborate in the truest sense. Cursor is not just another advancement in IDE technology; it's the prototype of the future development environment. One where the boundary between coder and code fades, replaced by a symbiotic relationship between human intent and machine execution.

Chapter 2

Getting Started with Cursor AI

System Requirements and Supported Platforms

Before diving into the capabilities of Cursor AI, it's crucial to understand the environments it supports and the technical specifications required to run it effectively. Cursor AI is designed to offer a seamless development experience enhanced by powerful artificial intelligence, and to accomplish this, certain system-level prerequisites must be met.

Cursor AI is a desktop-based IDE currently optimized for **macOS**, **Windows**, and

Linux. Its architecture is built to leverage both **local computation** and **cloud-based AI inference**, which means a balance between local performance and internet connectivity is required for a smooth experience.

Minimum System Requirements:

- **Operating System:**

  - macOS 12 (Monterey) or later

  - Windows 10 64-bit or later

  - Ubuntu 20.04 or later

- **Processor:**

- Intel Core i5 or AMD Ryzen 5 (quad-core minimum)

- Apple Silicon (M1, M2 chips fully supported)

- **Memory (RAM):**

  - 8GB RAM minimum (16GB recommended for optimal AI response times)

- **Storage:**

  - At least 2GB of free disk space for installation

- SSD storage recommended for better performance

- **Graphics:**

  - Integrated GPU is sufficient; no dedicated GPU required

- **Internet Connectivity:**

  - Stable internet connection required for AI queries, updates, and cloud sync features

Cursor is lightweight in terms of IDE requirements but powerful in functionality. For developers working in organizations with enterprise-grade security, additional considerations such as proxy configuration, VPN access, and data compliance standards may be relevant. Cursor does provide options for **self-hosted** or **enterprise deployments** for teams that require greater control over infrastructure.

Installation and Setup Process

Installing Cursor AI is straightforward, but the experience is enhanced by a guided setup that ensures you're ready to take advantage of its full suite of features. Depending on your operating system, installation may differ slightly.

macOS Installation:

1. Visit the official Cursor AI website and download the macOS .dmg installer.

2. Drag the Cursor app into the Applications folder.

3. On first launch, macOS Gatekeeper may prompt a security warning; approve the app from **System Preferences > Security & Privacy**.

4. Follow the onboarding wizard to sign in or create your Cursor account.

Windows Installation:

1. Download the `.exe` installer from the official Cursor AI website.

2. Run the installer and grant permission for administrative access.

3. The installation wizard will walk through the process; once complete, launch Cursor from the Start Menu or desktop shortcut.

4. Log in to your Cursor account to initialize AI services.

Linux Installation:

1. Download the `.AppImage` or `.deb` package depending on your

distribution.

2. For `.AppImage`, make it executable:

bash
CopyEdit
```
chmod +x cursor-x.y.z.AppImage
./cursor-x.y.z.AppImage
```

3. For `.deb`:

bash
CopyEdit
```
sudo dpkg -i cursor-x.y.z.deb

sudo apt-get install -f
```

4. Launch from the applications menu or command line.

Account Setup:

After installation, the next step is account registration. Cursor uses accounts to track preferences, manage projects, and authenticate access to the AI backend. You can sign up using:

- Email address

- GitHub account

- Google or other OAuth providers (if available)

Once authenticated, you'll be directed to choose your AI model preferences (GPT-4 or default settings), configure telemetry sharing (optional), and select your default workspace settings.

First Look at the Cursor AI Interface

Upon launching Cursor for the first time, the interface strikes a balance between minimalism and power. Borrowing design sensibilities from modern IDEs like VS Code, Cursor offers a clean and intuitive layout that's familiar to seasoned developers yet welcoming to newcomers.

Interface Breakdown:

- **Sidebar (Left Panel):**

- File Explorer: Displays your project's folder structure

- Search: Contextual search within your codebase

- Source Control: Git integration panel for versioning

- Extensions: Access to available plugins and tools

- AI Panel: Conversations and queries with Cursor's assistant

- **Editor Window (Center Pane):**

- This is the main canvas where you write and interact with your code.

- Cursor supports multiple tabs, split panes, and file navigation.

- **Command Palette:**

  - Activated by pressing `Cmd/Ctrl + Shift + P`, this lets you execute commands or search across features—such as invoking AI prompts, generating code snippets, or navigating projects.

- **AI Chat Window:**

- Integrated into the bottom panel or floating, the AI assistant acts like a co-developer.

- You can ask questions in natural language (e.g., "Explain this function" or "Generate a unit test for this file").

- **Status Bar (Bottom Panel):**

  - Displays project status, Git branch info, AI activity status, and environment info.

  - You can toggle AI features here or switch between light/dark modes.

- **Theme and Layout Customization:**

  - Cursor offers multiple themes, including popular ones like Monokai, Dracula, and Solarized.

  - Developers can customize layout docking, font sizes, line height, and keybindings according to their preferences.

Cursor's interface feels responsive, and its modular nature allows you to move panels around, making it highly adaptable to personal workflows.

Understanding the Onboarding Flow

The onboarding experience in Cursor is designed not just to get you started, but to set the tone for how you'll use the AI co-pilot in your workflow. It's more than a setup—it's a walkthrough of the future of coding.

Guided Tour and AI Activation:

Upon your first launch and login, Cursor initiates a **guided tour**. This takes you through:

1. **Project Setup:**

   ○ Open or create a project directory.

   ○ Cursor scans the files and loads the context for AI awareness.

2. **AI Assistant Introduction:**

- ○ You're introduced to the AI panel, where you can start chatting with Cursor.

- ○ A few sample prompts appear, like:

    - ■ "What does this function do?"

    - ■ "Can you suggest a better implementation for this loop?"

    - ■ "Generate TypeScript types from this JSON."

3. **AI Indexing:**

   ○ Cursor indexes your project files to provide intelligent responses.

   ○ Indexing ensures AI understands context like variable names, file structure, dependencies, and function definitions.

4. **Prompt Suggestions and Tips:**

   ○ A mini cheat-sheet appears showing useful natural language prompts.

   ○ Tips include how to reference code in the current file, multi-file queries, and using AI to debug errors.

5. **Interactive Tutorial (Optional):**

   ○ A small guided coding exercise walks you through writing a function, testing it, and optimizing it with AI suggestions.

   ○ You can skip or revisit this later under the Help menu.

Customization After Onboarding:

Once the initial tour is complete, you can fine-tune your environment:

- Set default AI model preferences (GPT-3.5, GPT-4, etc.)

- Enable/disable code indexing for specific folders (e.g., exclude `node_modules`)

- Manage your AI chat history and data privacy settings

- Configure keyboard shortcuts or integrate with GitHub/GitLab

Cursor is designed to meet you where you are. If you're a beginner, the onboarding flow offers just enough guidance to get comfortable. If you're experienced, you can breeze through it and immediately dive into customization and project-specific workflows.

To Conclude, Getting started with Cursor AI is an experience rooted in clarity and empowerment. From installation to the first AI-powered code suggestion, every interaction is tailored to reduce friction and increase productivity. The tool doesn't just aim to assist with coding, it aims to redefine how developers think, build, and iterate. Its cross-platform support, clean interface, and intelligent onboarding process ensure that whether you're an indie developer working on side projects or an enterprise engineer building large-scale systems, Cursor is ready to enhance your workflow from the very first line of code.

Chapter 3

Key Features and Capabilities

Cursor AI is a cutting-edge development companion that transforms how programmers write, analyze, and optimize their code. Its core features revolve around leveraging advanced AI models to improve productivity, reduce mental load, and enhance code quality.

AI-Assisted Code Suggestions

At the heart of Cursor AI is its intelligent code suggestion engine, designed to serve as your real-time coding assistant. Unlike traditional autocomplete features, Cursor AI's suggestions are powered by large language models, such as OpenAI's GPT-4, which understand programming languages, logic, structure, and even best practices.

How It Works

When you begin typing a function, comment, or control structure, Cursor analyzes the context of your file and project to predict what you're about to write next. It uses both your current input and surrounding code to generate suggestions that align with your intent. These suggestions aren't limited to completing variable names—they can include entire blocks of code, such as:

- Function templates

- API request handlers

- Error handling patterns

- Data transformations

- SQL queries or command-line snippets

Use Case Examples

- **Frontend Developers:** While writing a React component, Cursor might suggest props typing, JSX structure, and even event handling functions.

- **Backend Engineers:** While defining an Express.js route, it could automatically populate request validation, error checks, and response formatting.

- **Data Scientists:** When working in Python with pandas or NumPy, Cursor suggests data cleaning steps, aggregation methods, or graphing snippets using matplotlib or seaborn.

Customization Options

Developers can fine-tune the suggestion behavior by choosing the model version (GPT-3.5, GPT-4), adjusting the temperature for creativity, or enabling domain-specific context memory. Cursor also learns from your style over time, offering more relevant and personalized suggestions.

Intelligent Code Completion and Refactoring

Beyond simple suggestions, Cursor AI takes code completion and refactoring to a new level. These capabilities reduce the time spent on mundane tasks while ensuring the codebase stays clean, modular, and efficient.

Context-Aware Code Completion

Traditional IDEs offer symbol-based autocompletion. Cursor AI goes further with **semantic understanding**, meaning it reads and interprets the function and logic of your code. This allows it to:

- Predict next lines of code based on prior logic

- Suggest data transformations aligned with your code goals

- Complete partially written algorithms with optimal patterns

- Detect unused parameters and recommend removal

For instance, when writing a function that processes a CSV file, Cursor can suggest relevant parsing methods, header validations, and error handling that suit the use case.

Automated Refactoring Suggestions

Cursor AI identifies inefficient or outdated code patterns and recommends modern, maintainable alternatives. Examples of automated refactoring include:

- Extracting repeated logic into reusable functions

- Replacing nested if-else blocks with switch cases or guard clauses

- Optimizing loop constructs into list comprehensions or map/filter functions

- Suggesting object destructuring or optional chaining in JavaScript

Interactive Refactor Commands

With just a few keystrokes or a right-click, developers can invoke refactor suggestions.

Cursor provides a side-by-side preview of the refactored code and allows developers to approve, edit, or reject the changes. You can initiate commands such as:

- "Refactor this function for readability"

- "Make this method asynchronous"

- "Replace for-loop with a map function"

This intelligent refactor system reduces cognitive load while enforcing cleaner, modern code practices.

Documentation Generation

One of the most tedious but essential aspects of programming is writing documentation. Whether it's inline code comments, API references, or module explanations, documentation bridges the gap between code and comprehension. Cursor AI dramatically simplifies this process by generating documentation in real-time, tailored to the specific logic of your code.

Inline Docstring Generation

Cursor AI can automatically generate docstrings based on the function name, parameters, and expected behavior. It supports formats like:

- Google-style

- NumPy-style

- reStructuredText (for Sphinx)

- JSDoc (for JavaScript)

- TypeDoc (for TypeScript)

Example:

python
CopyEdit

```
def calculate_average(scores):
    """

    Calculate the average value
from a list of scores.

    Args:
```

```
    scores  (List[float]):  A
list of numerical scores.


    Returns:
        float: The average score.
    """ """ """
```

The AI not only inserts the format but fills in meaningful descriptions, saving time and improving consistency across your codebase.

API and Class-Level Documentation

Cursor AI also assists with generating module-level summaries and API guides. When working on REST APIs, it can scan routes and generate OpenAPI (Swagger) specifications. For object-oriented programming, it can describe the relationships between classes, methods, and inheritance hierarchies.

Markdown and Wiki Export

Documentation generated by Cursor can be exported directly into Markdown files, making it easy to sync with GitHub wikis, internal dev portals, or README files. This ensures your codebase is not just functional but also developer-friendly.

Test Writing and Error Detection

Quality assurance is integral to software development, and Cursor AI excels in helping developers write tests and spot bugs early in the process. It introduces automation without compromising accuracy, empowering you to build robust applications with confidence.

Unit and Integration Test Generation

Cursor AI can analyze your function logic and automatically generate unit tests for frameworks like:

- **Jest** (JavaScript/TypeScript)

- **PyTest** (Python)

- **JUnit** (Java)

- **RSpec** (Ruby)

- **Mocha/Chai** (Node.js)

Example prompt:

"Write tests for this Python function using PyTest."

The AI generates test cases for:

- Normal scenarios

- Edge cases

- Invalid inputs

- Exception handling

It even sets up test fixtures, mocks APIs, and asserts expected outcomes, reducing the time needed to manually write comprehensive test suites.

Error Identification and Debugging Suggestions

Cursor doesn't just catch syntax errors—it identifies **semantic and logical flaws** in your code, offering insights and fixes. While traditional linters flag rule violations, Cursor explains *why* the issue exists and *how* to fix it.

Common error detections include:

- Type mismatches

- Null/undefined access

- Misuse of async/await

- Unreachable code

- Shadowed variables

- Poor error propagation

Cursor provides inline suggestions and code fixes, optionally offering links to relevant documentation or Stack Overflow threads. For ambiguous logic, it suggests test-driven debugging: "Would you like me to write a test case for this?"

AI-Powered Static Analysis

By scanning entire projects, Cursor AI performs static analysis to detect performance bottlenecks, security risks (like SQL injection or XSS), and memory leaks. It recommends remediation strategies, making it a powerful addition to traditional CI pipelines.

In-Line Explanations and Contextual Insights

Cursor AI is like having a senior engineer embedded into your IDE, always ready to explain unfamiliar code, break down logic, or provide contextual learning without switching tabs.

On-Demand Code Explanation

Simply highlight a code block and ask, "Explain this code," and Cursor responds with a detailed, natural-language breakdown. It interprets:

- Functionality

- Algorithmic purpose

- Variable roles

- Dependencies

- Runtime behavior

This feature is especially useful for onboarding new developers, revisiting legacy code, or reviewing external contributions.

Real-Time Learning Aid

Cursor acts as a contextual tutor. If you're unsure about a piece of code, you can ask questions like:

- "What does this regex pattern do?"

- "Why is this loop running infinitely?"

- "How does this recursive call terminate?"

Instead of abstract textbook definitions, it explains the concepts using your actual code as a teaching material, personalized and practical.

Inline Tooltips and Hover Insights

When you hover over variables, functions, or imported modules, Cursor shows smart tooltips that include:

- Type information

- Definition references

- Usage examples

- Parameter details

It also surfaces warnings or recommendations dynamically. For example, if a parameter is unused or a function is too large, a subtle tooltip nudges you to refactor or comment.

Code History and Thought Process

One unique feature is the ability to ask Cursor: "Why was this change made?" If version control is enabled and commits are annotated well, Cursor can summarize the intent behind changes. This acts like a living changelog and helps future maintainers understand the evolution of the codebase.

Cursor AI reimagines the development process by integrating AI into the very fabric of coding. It doesn't just offer tools—it provides capabilities that act as an extension of the developer's mind. From intelligent suggestions and automated documentation to error detection and real-time explanations, every feature is purpose-built to amplify productivity and deepen understanding.

Whether you're building a solo project, contributing to open source, or leading a team in an enterprise setting, Cursor AI becomes a powerful ally in your development journey. It simplifies complexity, enhances code quality, and offers continuous support throughout the coding lifecycle.

Chapter 4

The Architecture Behind Cursor AI

Behind Cursor AI's sleek and responsive interface lies a sophisticated architecture that seamlessly blends AI intelligence with the robust functionality of a modern IDE. Understanding this architecture gives users insight into how Cursor operates in real-time, manages performance, ensures security, and delivers the rapid, high-quality assistance that defines it.

Integration with Large Language Models (Like GPT)

Cursor AI is deeply rooted in the capabilities of large language models (LLMs), particularly OpenAI's GPT series. These models power the natural language understanding, code synthesis, refactoring suggestions, explanations, and even documentation generation within the IDE.

Architecture Overview

At its core, Cursor functions as a hybrid architecture that combines local development tools with cloud-based LLM inference. When a user triggers an AI-powered action—such as asking for a code suggestion or explanation— Cursor collects relevant code context (within file, project, or prompt), packages it as a query, and securely sends it to the GPT API endpoint.

The response returned by the model is parsed, cleaned, and embedded directly into the editor in a contextual and formatted manner. This entire round-trip typically occurs within a second or two, designed to feel as responsive as local autocompletion.

Context Window and Prompt Engineering

One of the most critical components in this integration is the dynamic construction of prompts. Cursor AI carefully selects surrounding code (including imports, function definitions, file headers, and comments) to build a concise but informative context window. This allows GPT models to:

- Understand the user's intent

- Predict valid code continuations

- Generate relevant tests or docstrings

- Offer meaningful explanations

Cursor dynamically adjusts the size of the prompt window based on available model limits (such as 16k or 32k tokens), ensuring the LLM receives maximum context without hitting memory caps.

Model Choice and Fine-Tuning

Cursor supports multiple model backends, allowing users to choose between GPT-3.5, GPT-4, Claude, and other models. In some cases, Cursor leverages fine-tuned or domain-optimized models for tasks like refactoring, test writing, or generating documentation for specific languages.

This flexibility ensures that users can optimize for speed, cost, or quality depending on their preferences and the task at hand.

How AI Agents Work in Real Time Within the IDE

The real power of Cursor AI lies not just in static model queries but in its real-time AI agents—autonomous components that operate within the IDE to assist with ongoing tasks, from writing and reviewing code to managing files and integrating documentation.

Event-Driven AI Agents

Cursor's agents are event-driven and context-sensitive. They monitor your actions—typing, saving, hovering, or highlighting—and anticipate where help might be needed. These agents are non-intrusive and work silently in the background, surfacing only when relevant.

For example:

- **Typing Code:** As you write, the Completion Agent offers suggestions.

- **Highlighting Code:** The Explanation Agent becomes available for instant clarification.

- **Opening a PR:** The Review Agent summarizes changes and suggests improvements.

- **Creating a Test File:** The Test Agent scans the source and proposes test coverage.

These agents operate asynchronously and are optimized to avoid blocking the user's workflow, relying on efficient multi-threading and message queues to handle user interactions smoothly.

Contextual Awareness

Unlike static linters or autocomplete engines, Cursor's agents maintain **multi-layered context**:

- **File Context:** Code in the current file

- **Project Context:** Dependencies, package files, and architecture

- **Historical Context:** Recently written or modified code

- **Prompt Context:** User queries or commands

This context stack enables AI agents to understand not just *what* you're writing but *why*, allowing for deeper and more relevant assistance.

Autonomous Workflows

Cursor supports multi-step AI workflows through chained agent operations. For instance, when writing a test:

1. The user writes a function.

2. The Test Agent detects the new function and generates candidate tests.

3. The Refactor Agent optimizes the test code for readability.

4. The Documentation Agent annotates the test file with usage notes.

These workflows are modular, allowing developers to accept, reject, or revise each stage independently.

Cursor's Design Philosophy: Local Tools + AI Assistance

One of the standout principles behind Cursor's design is the **combination of local development tools with powerful AI assistance**. Rather than replacing traditional tooling, Cursor enhances and integrates with it.

Why This Matters

Purely cloud-based AI tools often suffer from latency, security concerns, and lack of integration with real projects. Conversely, offline tools lack the intelligence and flexibility of AI. Cursor solves this by adopting a hybrid architecture that offers:

- **Local Speed and Familiarity:** Code editing, linting, building, and formatting occur locally using native tooling like ESLint, Prettier, Black, or clang-format.

- **Cloud Intelligence:** AI queries, code explanations, and test generation are offloaded to the cloud, ensuring high-quality language understanding and synthesis.

This hybrid approach allows developers to retain control, leverage existing workflows, and use AI as an augmentation—not a replacement.

Extensibility and Plugin Support

Cursor is built on a modular foundation, enabling it to integrate with popular development stacks:

- **Version Control:** Native Git and GitHub integration

- **Package Managers:** npm, pip, Cargo, etc.

- **Linters & Formatters:** ESLint, Flake8, Prettier, Black

- **Build Tools:** Webpack, Make, Gradle, Vite

These integrations allow Cursor to work like a traditional IDE when needed, while infusing intelligence at every touchpoint. It's built for **incremental adoption**—you can start with a single AI feature and gradually expand.

Privacy and Developer Autonomy

Unlike some AI-enhanced platforms that automatically transmit your codebase to external servers, Cursor puts privacy and autonomy at the center. It clearly indicates when and what context is being sent to the model, and offers:

- Manual vs. automatic query submission

- Token usage tracking

- API key management

- Data exclusion zones (e.g., don't send .env or secrets folders)

Cursor ensures that developers remain in full control of their code and its exposure to AI systems.

Performance Optimization and Latency Management

For Cursor AI to deliver on its promise of real-time assistance, it must be fast. The architecture is optimized to reduce latency, balance load, and provide immediate feedback without freezing or stalling the editor.

Optimized Caching Layers

To reduce round-trip times to LLMs, Cursor employs:

- **Request Caching:** Frequent queries (like explaining popular functions or libraries) are cached locally and in-memory.

- **Prompt Deduplication:** Repeated prompts are deduplicated to avoid sending redundant queries.

- **Cold Start Reduction:** Active connections to model APIs are maintained during sessions to prevent delays.

These measures significantly lower response times and improve the snappiness of AI features.

Parallelization and Background Processing

Cursor's agents operate in background threads and worker processes, ensuring that the main UI thread is never blocked. This architecture is inspired by concurrent systems where long-running operations (e.g., generating tests or analyzing files) do not disrupt typing or navigation.

Background jobs are managed via intelligent scheduling queues, prioritized by:

- Urgency (e.g., live completions > documentation generation)

- Resource intensity

- User activity (idle time = more background tasks)

Network Optimization

Cursor minimizes bandwidth usage by:

- Compressing payloads

- Sending diffs instead of entire files

- Using delta updates in long sessions

For teams working in remote environments or over VPNs, Cursor remains highly usable without demanding high-speed internet.

Model Selection for Performance

Not all tasks require the power (or latency) of GPT-4. Cursor smartly selects between models based on:

- **Task complexity:** GPT-3.5 for simple completions, GPT-4 for refactoring or explanations.

- **User preference:** Developers can set default models per feature.

- **Fallback mechanisms:** If GPT-4 is down, Cursor automatically falls back with a warning.

This adaptive selection ensures the right tradeoff between speed and accuracy.

Cursor AI's architecture is a prime example of modern software engineering, blending the best of local development environments with the intelligence of large-scale AI. Its seamless integration with LLMs, intelligent agent framework, and hybrid design philosophy make it not just a tool—but a platform for the future of software development.

By maintaining fast performance, respecting user control, and intelligently managing resources, Cursor AI achieves a rare balance: it is both powerful and practical. As developers continue to demand more intelligent, efficient, and trustworthy tools, Cursor sets the standard for what an AI-powered IDE should be.

Chapter 5

AI Pair Programming in Practice

The concept of pair programming that is two developers working side by side to write and refine code has long been a staple of agile development practices. Cursor AI takes this to a new level by introducing an AI-powered partner into the workflow. This AI assistant is always available, context-aware, non-intrusive, and capable of supporting everything from brainstorming to debugging.

Collaborating with Cursor's AI Assistant

At the heart of AI pair programming is the interaction between the developer and Cursor's AI assistant. This is not a rigid command-prompt system—it's a fluid collaboration where the AI acts more like a knowledgeable peer who reads code, understands context, and offers suggestions or guidance in natural language.

Interaction Styles

Cursor supports various interaction models depending on the user's needs and preferences:

- **Inline Suggestions**: As you write code, the AI suggests autocompletions, improvements, and best practices directly in the editor.

- **Natural Language Prompts**: You can highlight code and ask questions like, *"What's wrong with this logic?"* or *"Can you optimize this function?"*

- **Sidebar Chat**: A dedicated assistant panel allows for back-and-forth dialogue, where users can submit broader questions, troubleshoot issues, or request entire code snippets or designs.

This multi-modal communication allows users to choose how to engage—whether through commands, code annotations, or conversational prompts.

Task-Oriented Collaboration

Cursor's assistant is capable of breaking down complex programming tasks into manageable pieces and guiding you through them. Examples include:

- **Writing a New Feature**: You describe the functionality in plain English, and the AI offers a file structure, helper methods, and initial implementations.

- **Refactoring Legacy Code**: The AI analyzes the function or class, explains what's outdated or redundant, and rewrites the code with modern patterns.

- **Learning a New Library**: You ask the assistant to explain how to use

Tailwind CSS, or set up a GraphQL API, and it walks you through the integration with working code.

Over time, Cursor becomes like a second brain for the developer—quickly surfacing relevant information, managing boilerplate, and reducing the cognitive load of repetitive tasks.

Live Debugging and Problem-Solving with AI

One of the most compelling uses of Cursor AI is during live debugging sessions. Rather than searching through documentation, reading logs, or scouring Stack Overflow, developers can rely on Cursor's AI to diagnose, explain, and suggest fixes for code issues in real time.

Error Identification

When an error is detected—whether from a failing test, compiler message, or exception traceback—Cursor's AI can help interpret the message and locate the issue. For example:

- If a `TypeError` occurs, the AI can analyze the stack trace, infer the mismatch, and suggest a corrected call signature.

- If a function causes unintended side effects, the assistant might recommend an architectural fix like immutability or encapsulation.

Unlike static linters, Cursor offers **intelligent diagnostics** that take surrounding context, history, and project structure into account.

Interactive Debugging Workflow

A typical debugging workflow with Cursor might look like this:

1. You encounter an error in your code.

2. You highlight the problematic section and ask, *"Why am I getting this null value here?"*

3. The AI explains the possible root causes, walks through the execution path, and points out an uninitialized variable.

4. It suggests a fix—e.g., adding a conditional check or setting a default value.

5. You apply the fix, and the AI can optionally generate a test to validate the behavior.

This tight feedback loop dramatically reduces the time between encountering a problem and deploying a fix, enhancing productivity and reducing context switching.

AI-Assisted Logging and Instrumentation

Cursor can also assist with proactive debugging. For complex functions, you can request the AI to insert meaningful log statements, set up assertions, or even generate profiling tools to catch bottlenecks.

For example:

- "Add logging to trace the API response flow."

- "Insert a guard clause for the user input validation."

Cursor not only writes the code—it explains why certain logs are helpful, or how a conditional structure improves reliability.

Practical Use Cases and Sample Workflows

To help understand how Cursor functions in real-world development, it's useful to explore concrete workflows that developers regularly perform.

1. Feature Development from Scratch

Scenario: You need to build a new signup form using React.

Workflow:

- You prompt Cursor: *"Build a responsive signup form with email, password, and confirm password fields using React."*

- The AI generates the JSX structure, handles state using hooks, and adds basic validation.

- You ask: *"Add Tailwind CSS styles."*
  Cursor updates the code with styled
  classes.

- You request: *"Add a unit test for form
  validation."* Cursor provides a Jest test
  suite.

2. Refactoring and Modernizing Code

Scenario: You inherit a legacy class-based
React component and need to convert it to
functional syntax.

Workflow:

- You paste the code and ask Cursor:
  *"Convert this class component to a
  functional component using hooks."*

- Cursor rewrites the component using `useState` and `useEffect`.

- You follow up: *"Remove unused imports and simplify logic."*

- Cursor refactors further, reducing lines and improving readability.

3. Onboarding and Understanding a Codebase

Scenario: You're joining a new project and need to understand the backend routing.

Workflow:

- You open the routes file and ask: *"Explain what this file does."*

- Cursor analyzes the file, describes each route handler, and explains dependencies.

- You ask: *"How does the middleware authentication work here?"*

- Cursor traces the middleware and breaks down the auth flow.

This reduces the friction of onboarding and accelerates your ability to contribute meaningfully to new codebases.

4. Writing Tests for Legacy Code

Scenario: You need to improve test coverage on an older Python utility module.

Workflow:

- You open the module and ask: *"Write tests for these functions."*

- Cursor generates pytest-compatible test functions.

- You run the tests and find a failure.

- Cursor explains the cause and suggests a fix for the underlying bug.

Case Studies from Developer Experiences

To showcase the impact of Cursor's AI pair programming, here are brief case studies from developers across various industries.

Case Study 1: Startup Speed Boost

Profile: A small fintech startup building a React and Node.js web app.

Challenge: Deliver features quickly with a lean team.

Solution: The team integrated Cursor AI into their development flow. Instead of relying on boilerplate templates or copy-pasting code from documentation, they used the AI to scaffold features, write validation logic, and generate tests.

Result: Feature development time decreased by 40%. Developers reported higher satisfaction due to reduced repetitive work and more focus on logic and UI.

Case Study 2: Legacy Code Overhaul

Profile: An enterprise Java team modernizing a decade-old codebase.

Challenge: Migrating from Java 8 to Java 17 and applying modern design patterns.

Solution: Cursor was used to explain old code, suggest modern syntax, and refactor large classes. AI assistance helped with writing tests for previously untested modules.

Result: The migration was completed two months ahead of schedule. Test coverage increased from 58% to 84%, and bugs in production were reduced significantly.

Case Study 3: Educational Use

Profile: A computer science professor using Cursor in a classroom setting.

Challenge: Helping students understand code concepts while reducing reliance on teaching assistants.

Solution: Cursor was used to assist students during lab sessions. Students could ask the AI to explain loops, functions, and data structures in real time.

Result: Students reported faster comprehension and more confidence. The professor used Cursor to auto-generate practice problems and coding assignments.

AI pair programming is no longer a concept of the future—it's a reality that's reshaping how software is written, tested, and understood. With Cursor, developers gain a tireless partner that writes with them, thinks alongside them, and offers instant support. From writing features and debugging issues to onboarding quickly and modernizing legacy systems, Cursor AI elevates every stage of the development cycle.

Chapter 6

Customizing Your AI Workflow

While Cursor AI delivers powerful out-of-the-box functionality, its true potential lies in how well it adapts to your unique development workflow. No two developers or teams code exactly the same way—some prefer concise suggestions, others want verbose explanations; some focus on speed, others on clarity and reusability. Cursor understands this variability and allows for deep customization to create a tailored, efficient, and productive experience. This chapter explores how to mold the Cursor AI assistant to your specific needs by fine-tuning prompts, modifying code tone, creating reusable templates, and configuring personal or team-wide settings.

Tailoring Prompts for Different Coding Needs

The cornerstone of effective AI collaboration is how you phrase your prompts. Cursor allows developers to use natural language instructions to guide the assistant's behavior, and refining your prompt strategy can significantly improve output quality.

Prompting for Clarity, Optimization, or Speed

Depending on your goal, the way you ask for assistance can yield drastically different results:

- **Clarity-Focused Prompts**: If you want readable and maintainable code, use instructions like:

    - "Rewrite this function to be easier to understand."

    - "Add comments to explain each step of this algorithm."

- **Performance-Oriented Prompts**: For optimizing bottlenecks, instruct with:

- "Optimize this loop for speed."

- "Reduce memory usage in this image processing code."

- **Quick-and-Dirty Drafting**: When speed matters more than polish, say:

  - "Give me a fast draft implementation of a REST API with Express."

  - "Just generate working code, I'll clean it up later."

By clarifying intent in the prompt, you shape how the AI balances speed, elegance, and reliability.

Contextual Prompting

Cursor is context-aware, meaning it can incorporate surrounding code, project structure, and previous interactions into its suggestions. However, the clarity of your input still matters. The best practice includes:

- Highlighting the exact code you want help with.

- Including file-level context if asking about interdependencies.

- Providing short inline comments to guide the AI.

Examples:

- "Refactor this function to follow single-responsibility principle."

- "Based on this model class, create a corresponding serializer."

Being specific and contextual avoids generic outputs and aligns results with your intentions.

Adjusting AI Verbosity and Code Tone

Different projects have different standards when it comes to code verbosity, naming conventions, formatting, and commenting. Cursor gives you the ability to adjust how the AI communicates and presents its output.

Controlling Output Verbosity

You can direct Cursor to generate:

- **Verbose code**: More comments, expanded logic, longer but clearer expressions.

- **Concise code**: Fewer comments, one-liners, use of shorthand syntax.

Examples:

- "Write a verbose version with comments for junior devs."

- "Give a compact implementation for experienced team members."

This is useful when collaborating across skill levels or when working on open-source projects where clarity is key.

Setting a Tone for Naming Conventions

Cursor can adjust naming conventions based on your project's preferences:

- CamelCase vs snake_case

- Singular vs plural forms

- Verb-based function names (e.g., `getUserData`) vs noun-based (`userDataFetcher`)

You can guide this with prompts like:

- "Follow snake_case for all variables."

- "Use functional programming style for naming."

Cursor also learns over time from your feedback. If you repeatedly overwrite or reject a specific naming pattern, it gradually adapts to mirror your style.

Adjusting Commenting Style

Developers may prefer:

- **Inline comments** for specific lines.

- **Block comments** summarizing large sections.

- **Docstrings** following a specific format (e.g., JSDoc, Google, or NumPy style).

Cursor can generate or rewrite documentation in your chosen format. You can prompt it with:

- "Use NumPy-style docstring for this Python function."

- "Add JSDoc comments to this React component."

Over time, this standardizes your documentation style across the project.

Creating Reusable Templates and Scripts

For recurring patterns like test structures, API endpoint scaffolding, or component boilerplates, Cursor enables the creation and reuse of prompt-based templates that save time and enforce consistency.

Creating Code Templates

Cursor allows you to save and reuse prompt templates for:

- Unit tests

- CRUD APIs

- Service classes

- UI components

Example template prompt:

"Generate a RESTful API controller for [ModelName] with GET, POST, PUT, and DELETE routes using Express and TypeScript. Include basic validation and error handling."

You can save this and reuse it across different models or projects by just replacing the `[ModelName]`.

Reusable Prompt Snippets

Cursor supports command-style shortcuts or reusable snippets that you can invoke from the command palette or through contextual menus. These snippets function similarly to code macros.

Examples:

- "Test generator"

- "Comment explainer"

- "React component boilerplate"

These can be customized, shared across a team, and version-controlled alongside your project.

Automating Project Scaffolding

Advanced users can combine Cursor's scripting ability with custom prompts to generate entire folder structures or service layers from a single instruction. Example:

- "Set up a new Flask module named `invoice` with model, routes, views, and templates."

Cursor can then generate multiple files with interlinked logic, saving hours of manual setup.

Configuring Personal and Team-Wide Settings

Cursor is highly customizable at both the individual and organizational level, allowing users to define behavior, feedback modes, permissions, and project-specific rules.

User Preferences and Settings

Under **Settings**, users can control:

- **Default prompt tone** (friendly, formal, concise)

- **Code format style** (integrated with Prettier, Black, or ESLint rules)

- **Suggestion frequency** (always on, passive, on command)

- **Autocomplete behavior** (inline suggestions vs popover prompts)

You can also configure:

- Editor themes and UI layout

- Keyboard shortcuts for AI interactions

- Memory retention (how much history the AI remembers per session)

These preferences are stored locally and synced across devices when signed in.

Team Workspace Settings

For collaborative environments, Cursor allows teams to enforce consistent AI behavior across members by configuring:

- **Shared prompt templates**

- **Coding standards** (naming, comment styles, error handling rules)

- **Project-specific behaviors** (e.g., always include logging, prefer async functions)

Admins can define these settings in a `.cursor-config.json` file stored in the root of the repository. This ensures all AI interactions conform to team policies, improving consistency and avoiding rework.

Role-Based AI Behavior

In team projects, users can assign roles to Cursor for different tasks:

- **Architect**: Focuses on design and project structuring.

- **Debugger**: Specializes in finding and fixing code issues.

- **Mentor**: Explains concepts with educational detail.

- **Executor**: Fast, concise code generation with minimal explanation.

You can assign a mode or role with a simple prefix in your prompt:

"@Debugger: Why is this function returning undefined?"

This helps streamline collaboration between Cursor and various team members working under different constraints.

Customizing Cursor AI's workflow transforms it from a general-purpose tool into a finely tuned productivity engine tailored to your development habits, team culture, and project goals. By learning to tailor prompts, adjust verbosity, create reusable patterns, and configure environment settings, you unlock deeper efficiency, precision, and creative flow. Whether you're a solo developer or managing an enterprise-level engineering team, these capabilities empower you to get more done with less friction—while ensuring every line of code aligns with your standards and vision.

Chapter 7

Cursor AI and Version Control

In modern software development, version control is more than a safety net—it's a foundational layer of collaboration, experimentation, and release management. Git, as the dominant system in this space, has been indispensable for developers across all environments. Cursor AI intelligently integrates Git into its IDE experience, streamlining every phase of version control with contextual AI support.

Seamless Git Integration

Cursor AI provides native Git integration directly within its interface, enabling developers to commit, branch, push, pull, and review changes without leaving the development environment. Unlike traditional Git plugins, Cursor goes beyond basic Git functionality by embedding AI into each interaction.

Real-Time Git Awareness

Cursor continuously tracks file changes, staged files, diffs, and commit histories. It visually highlights modified lines and provides intuitive shortcuts for staging and reviewing. Its Git sidebar offers a real-time overview of:

- Current branch and remote tracking

- Modified and staged files

- Commit history with inline diffs

- Revert, stash, and merge options

Cursor also automatically detects untracked files and recommends `.gitignore` updates based on file types and development patterns. For example, when it sees auto-generated `.env` or `.log` files, it may suggest:

> "Would you like to add `.env` to your `.gitignore` to avoid committing sensitive data?"

Integrated Command Line and Visual Git

While developers can use the GUI for basic operations, Cursor also embeds a terminal with Git pre-configured. This gives power users the flexibility of raw Git commands while still benefiting from AI enhancements like inline documentation or command explanations.

Example:

- Typing `git cherry-pick` into the terminal can prompt:

  "This command applies the changes introduced by an existing commit. Would you like a visual preview?"

This hybrid interface supports all user types— from novices learning Git to advanced DevOps engineers managing multiple branches.

Writing Better Commit Messages with AI

One of the most overlooked aspects of Git hygiene is the quality of commit messages. Clear, consistent commit messages help teams track changes, understand history, and debug regressions faster. Cursor AI offers intelligent commit assistance to elevate this often-neglected task.

Auto-Generated Commit Summaries

When you stage changes, Cursor can automatically analyze the diff and suggest a commit message. For example:

diff
CopyEdit

```
- Fixed typo in user authentication
method
+    Added    password    strength
validation logic
```

Cursor might suggest:

"Enhance password validation; fix typo in authentication module"

It follows best practices such as:

- Using imperative tone ("Add" instead of "Added")

- Grouping related changes

- Keeping messages concise and informative

You can customize templates, such as:

- Conventional commits (`feat:`, `fix:`, `chore:`)

- JIRA ticket integration (`[JIRA-123]`)

- Team-specific message styles

Commit Message Review and Rewrite

You can also ask the AI to rewrite a commit message to follow conventions or improve clarity:

"Rewrite the commit message to follow Conventional Commits format."

Cursor might change:

"fixed bug in form" to

```
fix(form): resolve form
submission validation error
```

It can also generate extended descriptions for multi-line commit messages, summarizing all staged changes in natural language.

Auto-Generating PRs and Summaries

Writing pull request (PR) descriptions can be tedious and inconsistent. Cursor AI automates this process by analyzing your branch's changes and generating detailed, structured PR summaries ready for GitHub, GitLab, or Bitbucket.

PR Title and Description Templates

When initiating a pull request, Cursor offers:

- A smart title summarizing the main change.

- A description including:

  - What was changed

  - Why it was changed

  - How to test it

- Any known issues or dependencies

Example: **Title**: `feat(auth):` `add` `password` `strength` `validator` `and` `update form UX`

Description:

This PR introduces password strength validation on the user registration form using a new helper method in `auth_utils.py`. It also updates the frontend UX to display real-time feedback. This resolves issue #112 and prepares for MFA rollout in phase 2.

Test Instructions:

1. Navigate to the registration form.

2. Enter a weak password and observe feedback.

3. Confirm backend rejection of insecure passwords.

AI Review of Code Diff Before PR Creation

Cursor's AI can also inspect your changes and alert you about:

- Redundant or unused code

- Forgotten TODOs

- Style inconsistencies

- Potential security concerns

Before you create the PR, Cursor might prompt:

> "This code uses an outdated hashing algorithm. Would you like to update it to `bcrypt`?"

These preemptive checks raise code quality and reduce post-PR feedback.

Managing Branches and Resolving Merge Conflicts

Branch management is another area where Cursor simplifies a traditionally complex workflow—especially when dealing with merge conflicts, rebases, and long-lived feature branches.

Branch Navigation and Visualization

Cursor offers a visual Git graph for managing branches, including:

- Current working branch

- Upstream and downstream dependencies

- Rebase and merge previews

- Fast-forward suggestions

You can rename, delete, or merge branches using the GUI or command line, with AI support to explain consequences before execution.

Example:

> "You are about to rebase `feature/login` onto `main`. This will replay your commits on top of the latest `main`. Shall I proceed?"

Conflict Detection and Resolution with AI Assistance

Merge conflicts are often frustrating and time-consuming. Cursor uses AI to detect, explain, and help resolve conflicts directly in the editor.

When a conflict arises, Cursor:

- Highlights the conflicting sections with contextual comments

- Explains what caused the conflict

- Suggests a merged version that preserves logic from both branches

Example:

diff

CopyEdit

```
<<<<<<< HEAD
return calculateTax(price);
=======
return           calculateTax(price,
region);
>>>>>>> feature/tax-update
```

Cursor might say:

> "Conflict detected: `calculateTax` function now expects an additional `region` parameter. Would you like to update the call in `HEAD` to include `region`?"

Then it offers an auto-merged version:

js
CopyEdit

```js
return calculateTax(price, region || 'default');
```

This drastically reduces the cognitive load and speeds up resolution.

Auto-Stashing and Conflict Recovery

Cursor also auto-stashes unsaved changes during risky operations like rebases or resets, ensuring you don't lose work. If something goes wrong, it will prompt:

> "Would you like to restore your previous state before the rebase?"

This safety net provides confidence when performing complex Git operations.

Cursor AI transforms the version control experience from a technical chore into a fluid, intelligent process. With Git deeply integrated into its core and AI woven through every stage—commit messages, PRs, branch handling, and conflict resolution—developers gain a powerful edge in managing code collaboration. By elevating the quality of your commits and reducing the friction of Git workflows, Cursor empowers individuals and teams to ship cleaner, faster, and more confidently.

Chapter 8

Advanced Use Cases and Integrations

As developers continue to build more complex, scalable, and collaborative systems, development environments must evolve to support diverse use cases, languages, and tools. Cursor AI rises to this challenge by offering seamless integration with external APIs, DevOps pipelines, databases, and multi-language projects—all while maintaining intelligent, context-aware AI support.

Integrating with APIs and External Tools

Modern development hinges on APIs and third-party services. Whether you're integrating Stripe for payments, Twilio for messaging, or internal REST/GraphQL endpoints, understanding and managing these integrations is often labor-intensive. Cursor AI simplifies this process by intelligently assisting with API exploration, request construction, response parsing, and integration testing.

API Documentation Parsing

Cursor can analyze API documentation, whether it's Swagger/OpenAPI, Postman collections, or even unstructured docs from a URL. Once identified, it can:

- Auto-generate client code in your language of choice

- Provide real-time suggestions as you write API requests

- Translate cURL requests into functional code snippets

For example:

> "You pasted a cURL request. Would you like me to generate an Axios or Fetch equivalent in JavaScript?"

It can even summarize endpoints:

> "This `/v1/users` endpoint requires an API key and returns user data with pagination."

Live API Interaction within the IDE

Cursor allows developers to run API calls within the IDE, either via integrated HTTP clients or through AI-generated request builders. When you draft a function like:

python
CopyEdit

```
def get_weather(city):
    # Call external weather API
```

Cursor might suggest:

> "You can use the OpenWeatherMap API. Here's a full implementation with API key management and error handling."

It also includes tools for managing secrets (e.g., `.env` handling), caching responses, and mocking services for testing.

Third-Party SDK Support and Integration

Cursor AI recognizes common third-party SDKs like Firebase, AWS, Stripe, etc. It provides:

- Auto-import suggestions

- Step-by-step usage help

- Error explanation and debug assistance

If a Stripe payment fails, Cursor can analyze the error object and suggest the fix:

"This error indicates an invalid currency format. Use USD instead of usdollars."

Cursor for DevOps and CI/CD Workflows

Cursor isn't just for writing code—it supports the full development lifecycle, including deployment, automation, and monitoring. With DevOps integrations, Cursor brings AI into build pipelines, container orchestration, and CI/CD configuration.

CI/CD Pipeline Support

Whether using GitHub Actions, GitLab CI, CircleCI, or Jenkins, Cursor can help generate and validate CI/CD configuration files. When

you create a new YAML file like
`.github/workflows/deploy.yml`, it can:

- Autocomplete workflow steps

- Validate syntax

- Explain runner settings and permission scopes

- Suggest environment-specific best practices

Example prompt:

> "I want to build, test, and deploy a Node.js app on every push to main."

Cursor might generate:

yaml

CopyEdit

```yaml
name: Deploy Node App
on:
  push:
    branches: [main]
jobs:
  build:
    runs-on: ubuntu-latest
    steps:
      - uses: actions/checkout@v2
      - name: Set up Node
        uses: actions/setup-node@v2
        with:
          node-version: '16'
```

```
- run: npm install

- run: npm test

- run: npm run deploy
```

Container and Infrastructure Tooling

Cursor supports Docker, Kubernetes, Terraform, and similar tools. It can:

- Auto generate Dockerfiles and `docker-compose.yml`

- Validate Kubernetes manifests

- Provide terraform module templates

- Interpret infrastructure logs and explain deployment errors

If your container fails to build, Cursor might highlight the failing step and suggest:

> "Looks like the `node_modules` folder is not in `.dockerignore`. This may cause build issues."

Monitoring and Observability Integration

Cursor can connect with logs or telemetry tools like Datadog, Sentry, or Prometheus. While it doesn't replace these platforms, it helps parse log output or visualize errors from the IDE:

> "You received a 502 error in production. The stack trace points to an expired database token. Would

you like help automating the renewal process?"

Multi-language Support and Switching Contexts

Today's applications are polyglot by nature—front-end in TypeScript, back-end in Go, scripts in Python, tests in Ruby. Cursor is built for this diversity, supporting context-aware AI across dozens of languages and enabling seamless context switching within the same project.

Language Detection and Switching

Cursor automatically detects the file type and programming language, tailoring its AI responses accordingly. For instance:

- JavaScript files receive web development-focused suggestions

- Python files benefit from scientific and ML library knowledge

- Java files include OOP structuring help and performance tips

When switching between files, the AI retains project context to offer cohesive suggestions. For example, if you define an API schema in a TypeScript file and consume it in a Python backend, Cursor understands the interface expectations and can adapt accordingly.

Cross-Language Refactoring

Cursor also enables transformations between languages. If you're migrating a utility function from Python to TypeScript, you can prompt:

"Convert this Python class to an equivalent in TypeScript with typed interfaces."

It ensures language-idiomatic output and follows the appropriate design patterns for the target language.

Testing Across Languages

Cursor supports multiple test frameworks and can auto-generate or refactor tests:

- Python: pytest, unittest

- JavaScript: Jest, Mocha

- Java: JUnit

- Go: go test

For each, it can provide:

- Boilerplate test setup

- Mocking/stubbing guidance

- Inference of test cases from implementation code

AI-Assisted Database Handling and Schema Management

Databases are a critical part of application architecture, and Cursor's AI support extends to schema design, query generation, ORM handling, and even migrations.

Schema Design Assistance

Cursor can help define database schemas based on model definitions or business requirements. If you write:

ts

CopyEdit

```
interface User {
  name: string;
  email: string;
  password: string;
}
```

Cursor can suggest:

> "Would you like to generate a
> PostgreSQL schema for this model?"

And return:

sql
CopyEdit

```sql
CREATE TABLE users (
  id SERIAL PRIMARY KEY,
  name VARCHAR(255),
  email VARCHAR(255) UNIQUE NOT
NULL,
  password VARCHAR(255) NOT NULL,
  created_at TIMESTAMP DEFAULT
CURRENT_TIMESTAMP
);
```

Query Writing and Optimization

Whether you're writing SQL queries directly or using ORMs like Sequelize, Prisma, or SQLAlchemy, Cursor can:

- Generate queries from natural language prompts

- Optimize slow queries

- Explain complex joins and subqueries

- Refactor raw queries into ORM syntax

Prompt:

"Get all users who haven't logged in for 30 days"

Response:

sql

CopyEdit

```sql
SELECT * FROM users WHERE
last_login < NOW() - INTERVAL '30
days';
```

Follow-up:

"Convert this to a Prisma query"

Response:

ts

CopyEdit

```ts
const inactiveUsers = await
prisma.user.findMany({
  where: {
```

```
lastLogin: {
  lt: subDays(new Date(), 30),
  },
 },
});
```

Database Migration Management

Cursor supports migration workflows for tools like Liquibase, Flyway, Prisma Migrate, and Django Migrations. It can:

- Generate migration scripts from schema diffs

- Explain each SQL operation

- Verify forward and backward compatibility

Example:

> "I changed `email` to `username` in the User model. Create a safe migration."

Cursor might respond:

sql
CopyEdit

```
ALTER TABLE users RENAME COLUMN email TO username;
```

With:

"This change is safe if you don't rely on an `email` index. Would you like me to check usage across the codebase?"

With advanced integration capabilities, Cursor AI extends far beyond traditional IDEs, supporting real-world software workflows with intelligence and precision. Whether you're integrating external APIs, managing DevOps pipelines, juggling multiple languages, or fine-tuning database schemas, Cursor becomes an indispensable AI collaborator. Its versatility empowers solo developers and teams alike to build, ship, and maintain modern applications faster—with fewer errors and more confidence.

Chapter 9

Debugging and Troubleshooting with Cursor

How Cursor Helps Detect Bugs

Cursor AI has revolutionized the debugging process by integrating real-time diagnostic capabilities directly into the developer's workflow. Unlike traditional debugging tools that require setting breakpoints, examining call stacks, or executing manual print statements, Cursor uses machine learning models to analyze code in real time and identify potential issues before they manifest into runtime errors. As you type, Cursor inspects your logic, control flow, and syntax patterns to catch edge cases and anti-patterns, highlighting potential bugs on the fly. These insights are often accompanied by inline annotations or suggestions that point out risky constructs and offer safer alternatives.

Cursor's ability to detect bugs stems from its large language model integration, trained on millions of code samples and bug reports. It compares your code against known problematic patterns and flags anomalies early. Additionally, it continuously learns from your interactions—correcting itself based on your accepted or ignored suggestions, thereby improving its accuracy over time.

Real-Time Suggestions for Bug Fixes

One of the most compelling features of Cursor is its capacity to offer bug fixes instantly. Once a problem is detected, Cursor doesn't just underline the issue—it suggests full or partial solutions. Whether it's an off-by-one error in a loop, a potential null pointer exception, or an incorrectly scoped variable, Cursor's fix suggestions come with explanations that help you understand why a particular solution works.

For instance, if you forget to handle an error from a function that returns a result and an error object in Go, Cursor might highlight the oversight and recommend wrapping the call in an `if err != nil` block, complete with an example of logging or returning the error gracefully. This speeds up the feedback loop dramatically, eliminating the need to compile and test multiple iterations manually.

Cursor also keeps track of related logic in surrounding code. If your bug involves a function that is used in several locations, the AI can propose fixes that apply across those instances consistently, helping to avoid regression bugs and inconsistencies. This holistic view streamlines the correction process and increases confidence in the stability of your changes.

Understanding AI's Reasoning Process

To build trust with developers, Cursor has invested in explainability. Each recommendation provided by the AI assistant can be accompanied by a rationale, enabling you to understand the 'why' behind the suggestion. This transparency demystifies the black-box nature of AI and fosters a collaborative relationship between the developer and the tool.

When you hover over or click on a suggestion, Cursor might present a brief explanation such as: "This loop may run one iteration too many due to inclusive boundary," or "This variable is declared but never used, which could indicate a logical error." These contextual insights are generated based on natural language processing combined with static code analysis.

The user interface often includes options to explore alternative fixes, accept the suggestion as-is, or ask for clarification. This back-and-forth mimics a real pair programming session where the junior developer asks questions and the senior partner explains concepts clearly. Over time, this dynamic builds the user's technical skills while also fine-tuning the AI's recommendations to better match the team's coding style and expectations.

Limitations and How to Override Incorrect Outputs

Despite its strengths, Cursor AI is not infallible. It may occasionally produce suggestions that are syntactically correct but semantically flawed. This typically occurs in edge cases where domain-specific logic or proprietary algorithms are in play—areas where the AI has limited contextual training.

One key limitation is that the AI might misinterpret the developer's intent, especially in codebases that use unconventional patterns or heavily rely on meta-programming. In such cases, the suggested fix may not only be irrelevant but could introduce new bugs. Developers must maintain a healthy skepticism and always review proposed changes critically.

Cursor provides mechanisms to override or ignore incorrect suggestions easily. You can dismiss recommendations, disable auto-suggestions for certain files or code blocks, or provide explicit instructions to the AI. For example, typing a comment like `// AI: ignore suggestion here` can suppress automated input in sensitive areas. This gives developers fine-grained control over when and where the AI assistant intervenes.

Another useful feature is feedback looping. If a suggestion is incorrect, you can flag it with a note explaining why it was unhelpful. Cursor uses this data to retrain and refine future outputs, making it less likely to repeat the same mistake. The tool also logs these interactions, allowing teams to review how the AI is being used and which areas require additional human oversight.

Cursor also offers the ability to roll back AI-applied changes. This version control-like feature ensures that you can experiment freely with AI suggestions without worrying about irreversible alterations to your codebase. It's an important safety net that balances innovation with accountability.

Ultimately, effective debugging with Cursor requires a partnership mindset. Developers should view the AI assistant not as a replacement for critical thinking but as a powerful collaborator that can spot issues faster, suggest solutions more broadly, and help maintain high code quality at scale.

Chapter 10

Security, Privacy, and Ethical Use

As developers increasingly adopt AI-powered tools like Cursor AI into their daily workflows, questions around security, privacy, and ethical usage have become more critical than ever. While the promise of automated intelligence revolutionizes productivity, it also raises nuanced considerations around data sharing, sensitive information handling, collaborative responsibilities, and legal obligations surrounding AI-generated code.

Local vs. Cloud Processing: What's Shared and What's Private

A core concern for developers working on proprietary or sensitive projects is the extent to which their code is exposed during AI interactions. Cursor AI addresses this by offering both **local processing capabilities** and **cloud-based AI model integrations**, depending on the task, configuration, and user preferences.

Understanding Local Execution

Cursor's architecture prioritizes privacy by allowing certain operations—like syntax highlighting, file management, or local linting—to remain completely on-device. This ensures that common editing actions do not leave the local environment, reducing the risk of data exposure.

For teams working under strict data governance policies—such as those in healthcare, finance, or defense sectors—this local-first architecture provides peace of mind. Cursor makes it transparent which processes are kept local, and users can further isolate projects through private workspace settings, limiting any potential leakage of data.

Cloud-Based AI Interactions

When AI features like code generation, natural language explanations, or large context analysis are invoked, some information may be sent to cloud-based models, typically via secure APIs connected to LLM providers such as OpenAI's GPT. Cursor uses encrypted HTTPS transmission and adheres to data minimization principles—only sending the code fragments necessary for completing the user's request.

Importantly, Cursor does not store any code permanently unless explicitly enabled by the user or organization for telemetry or logging purposes. Users can also view and manage what data is being transmitted in real time through the transparency dashboard in settings, offering complete visibility into their AI interactions.

Best Practices for Handling Sensitive Code

To reduce the risks associated with AI-involved workflows, developers and organizations should follow a robust set of best practices when dealing with confidential or mission-critical codebases.

Enable Safe Mode in Sensitive Environments

Cursor includes a "Safe Mode" toggle that disables all remote interactions. Developers working within air-gapped networks or government-restricted environments should default to this setting to ensure zero communication with external servers. Additionally, Cursor supports full offline coding, letting users temporarily disconnect cloud services without disrupting core IDE functionality.

Redact or Obfuscate Before Prompting

Before sending code snippets to AI models, users should redact or mask sensitive tokens, credentials, or proprietary algorithm logic. Cursor includes a built-in masking tool that can automatically detect and replace identifiable strings like API keys or database passwords before external processing.

Use Workspace-Specific Permissions

For enterprise users, Cursor enables role-based access control (RBAC) and workspace-level settings to restrict who can use AI features on what repositories. Sensitive internal tools can be isolated from cloud-enabled AI, while less critical projects benefit from full automation.

Keep Logs Encrypted and Localized

While Cursor allows logging for audit trails and debugging, it supports encrypted log storage and local-only retention policies. Developers should ensure that log files do not contain sensitive code excerpts and are stored securely according to organizational standards.

The Responsibility of Using AI in Team Environments

Collaboration is one of Cursor's strengths, especially in teams working across geographies and skill levels. However, with great power comes greater responsibility, particularly when AI is involved in generating, modifying, or interpreting code collaboratively.

AI as a Collaborator, Not a Replacement

Cursor's AI assistant is designed to **augment** human developers—not replace them. In team environments, it's vital to frame the AI as a suggestion engine rather than an authoritative source. Code produced through Cursor should always undergo peer review and approval processes before being merged into production.

Developers must remain vigilant and verify the correctness, security, and style of AI-generated content. While Cursor often produces syntactically correct and contextually accurate output, it can occasionally suggest insecure or non-performant solutions that require human scrutiny.

Establishing Review Workflows

To manage the influence of AI in collaborative repositories, teams should establish explicit workflows such as:

- **Mandatory AI-generated code tagging**, to identify suggestions derived from LLMs.

- **Automated linters and vulnerability scanners** integrated with pull requests.

- **Shared prompt history**, enabling teammates to audit past AI interactions.

Cursor facilitates many of these processes with GitHub and GitLab integrations, commit annotation features, and team-specific prompt histories.

Managing AI Interactions in Pair Programming

In AI-pair programming scenarios, Cursor often assumes the role of a co-developer. This makes it critical for teams to communicate clearly when reviewing contributions. Clear labeling of AI-generated code helps distinguish between human-written and machine-suggested logic, reducing ambiguity during handoffs and minimizing unintentional propagation of AI-induced bugs or inconsistencies.

Navigating License Implications with AI-Generated Code

One of the murkiest legal areas in modern development is the question of who owns code created by AI—and what obligations developers have when using such code in commercial applications.

Understanding the Legal Landscape

Most AI models, including those integrated with Cursor, are trained on a large corpora of publicly available code. This includes open-source repositories with varying licenses— MIT, GPL, Apache, and others. While model providers attempt to scrub or anonymize data, it's still possible for AI to generate snippets that closely resemble copyrighted code.

This raises concerns around derivative works, license compliance, and intellectual property (IP) rights, especially in commercial environments.

Cursor's Position and Disclaimers

Cursor clearly outlines in its terms of service that AI-generated suggestions are provided **"as-is"** and may not carry guarantees of originality. It recommends that users treat AI-generated code as a draft or starting point and apply the same diligence they would with any third-party library or snippet.

Cursor does not assume ownership of generated code, nor does it provide warranty against infringement. This means the burden of legal compliance rests with the developer or organization using the tool.

Best Practices for Legal Safety

To protect yourself and your organization:

- **Always vet AI-generated code** for similarities to known libraries or frameworks.

- **Use attribution or comments** when incorporating AI-assisted code into projects, especially if it mimics an existing API or interface.

- **Run license compliance tools** such as FOSSA, Snyk, or WhiteSource on final codebases to flag issues.

- **Avoid relying solely on AI for implementing complex or novel algorithms**, especially when those implementations could have originated from copyrighted open-source code.

Team-Level Governance

Larger organizations should create internal policies outlining acceptable use of AI-generated code. This may include restricting its use in certain projects, enforcing attribution standards, or requiring legal review before publishing software derived with AI assistance.

Cursor offers admin-level controls for team governance, including prompt moderation, logging of AI interaction history, and disabling model access in high-risk contexts.

Security, privacy, and ethical use are not afterthoughts—they are foundational to responsible development in the age of AI. Cursor AI offers a well-balanced ecosystem that respects developer autonomy while integrating powerful automation tools. By understanding where and how data is processed, applying best practices for secure coding, maintaining transparency in team environments, and complying with license requirements, developers can confidently embrace the benefits of AI without compromising their integrity or their users' trust.

The evolution of IDEs with AI like Cursor isn't just about speeding up code; it's about reimagining what it means to build software responsibly, intelligently, and ethically. When used with care and accountability, tools like Cursor not only enhance productivity but also elevate the standards of modern software engineering.

Chapter 11

Productivity Tips and Best Practices

Mastering Keyboard Shortcuts and Efficient Navigation

Efficiency begins at your fingertips. Cursor AI is designed to keep your hands on the keyboard and your focus in the code. Mastering keyboard shortcuts is not just about saving a few seconds—it's about entering a state of flow where coding becomes frictionless. Cursor offers an extensive range of shortcuts that help you traverse files, trigger AI actions, search documentation, and execute commands with precision.

Keybindings for navigating between files, switching tabs, and jumping to function definitions eliminate the need to rely on your mouse or trackpad. For example, jumping between definitions using simple key combinations or searching through code files without leaving your main editor screen transforms how quickly you move through tasks. Additionally, Cursor supports customization of shortcuts, allowing you to map actions to keys that best suit your muscle memory.

Cursor's quick action bar is another gem. Triggered by a shortcut, it allows developers to issue commands like "Refactor this function," "Generate test," or "Explain this code," all without interrupting their rhythm. Leveraging these features helps prevent productivity drains caused by clunky, manual operations.

Building Daily Routines with AI to Maximize Output

The most productive developers don't just work hard—they work smart by integrating AI into their daily flow. Cursor becomes a personal assistant that helps you plan, write, review, and refine your code as part of a structured routine.

Start your day with AI-driven planning. Feed Cursor a high-level goal or ticket description, and it can help scaffold your approach— suggesting folder structures, module names, and initial code outlines. During implementation, allow AI to handle the repetitive tasks like boilerplate generation, formatting, and function skeletons.

Develop a daily ritual of AI-assisted code reviews. Once a block of logic is implemented, prompt Cursor to analyze it, flag possible errors, or suggest refactors. Use the AI not only to write but to review your thinking— prompt it with questions like "Is there a more efficient way to do this?" or "Is this the cleanest implementation?"

Another powerful daily habit is using AI for retrospective summaries. Ask Cursor to summarize the day's code changes, draft commit messages, or create documentation. This habit keeps your repository clean and your brain less burdened by admin tasks, leaving more cognitive room for innovation and logic structuring.

Reducing Context-Switching through Smart Commands

One of the greatest hidden killers of productivity is context-switching. Moving from code to browser, to terminal, to docs, then back to code, costs mental energy. Cursor is engineered to consolidate these touchpoints into a single environment.

Instead of leaving your IDE to Google a function, highlight it and ask Cursor to explain or document it. Rather than opening a browser tab for Stack Overflow, ask Cursor to solve your bug, propose a fix, or reframe your logic. With these smart commands embedded directly in your workflow, you remain in a continuous cognitive thread, reducing the recovery time between tasks.

Cursor also allows you to anchor certain interactions in side panels, so documentation, suggestions, or AI chats are always just a glance away. You no longer need to dig through tabs or windows—the assistant is context-aware and responds relative to the code you're actively writing or inspecting.

Smart commands also extend to terminal tasks. Instead of mentally shifting gears to remember shell syntax, you can describe your intention—like "List all Docker containers" or "Search for a string in all files"—and let Cursor convert it to the appropriate command. This natural-language-to-command conversion significantly reduces the barrier to interacting with your project infrastructure.

Combining Cursor with Other Productivity Tools

While Cursor is powerful on its own, it becomes exponentially more useful when integrated into your broader productivity stack. Developers who pair Cursor with project management, communication, and deployment tools experience smoother workflows and fewer dropped threads.

For example, integrating Cursor with GitHub or GitLab lets you automate pull requests, update branches, and generate summaries. Use the AI to write concise PR descriptions based on your commit history or have it auto-summarize file diffs in a human-readable format. This streamlines communication with team members and enhances your ability to ship high-quality code faster.

If you use tools like Notion, Trello, or Jira, Cursor can help bridge the gap between planning and execution. With plugins or simple copy-paste actions, Cursor can convert Jira tickets into code stubs or generate structured plans based on Notion documentation. This tight loop ensures you're always working toward the original requirement without veering off-track.

Cursor also works well with note-taking tools like Obsidian or Evernote. After a coding session, export AI-generated summaries or architecture decisions into your documentation system for long-term knowledge sharing. The habit of "working with traceability" becomes painless when Cursor does most of the heavy lifting.

Finally, for CI/CD pipelines, Cursor can help script deployment processes, generate YAML files, and debug failed builds by analyzing logs in real-time. You no longer have to switch into DevOps mode completely—Cursor brings the needed intelligence into your development frame.

Maximizing Focus and Output with Cursor Workflows

To truly harness Cursor's productivity power, developers must view it as a thought partner rather than a passive tool. This shift enables a workflow where AI augments your thinking, suggests new possibilities, and reduces the number of micro-decisions required per coding session.

Adopt a habit of pairing with Cursor at key moments: project initiation, complex problem solving, refactor checkpoints, and end-of-day retros. Create reusable prompt templates for each of these stages, so you don't have to remember what to ask or how to phrase it. Templates such as "Suggest a module layout for this feature," "Optimize this function for speed," or "Generate docs for this class" save time and maintain quality.

Encourage team-wide alignment by documenting best AI prompt practices. Set prompt standards, such as always specifying language, framework, and desired tone when asking for documentation. By standardizing your team's interaction with Cursor, you create consistent outputs and reduce onboarding time for new developers.

Establish a feedback loop with Cursor by correcting its errors or suggesting alternative implementations. The AI learns from contextual corrections, and these exchanges improve its ability to serve you effectively in future tasks.

Sustaining Momentum and Avoiding Burnout

Another overlooked dimension of productivity is sustainability. Cursor helps maintain a steady pace without overburdening you with cognitive load. By outsourcing the repetitive, predictable, or mentally draining tasks to AI, developers conserve their focus for the challenges that matter.

Use Cursor to manage mental load during long coding sessions. Let it summarize where you left off, generate TODO lists, or outline next steps before you log off. The next time you return, Cursor becomes your memory—reminding you of context and re-orienting you swiftly.

Cursor also offers a more humane coding experience. By offloading mechanical thinking, it leaves you more bandwidth to be creative, thoughtful, and deliberate in your approach. This is especially helpful during high-pressure sprints or deadline crunches, where burnout is a real risk.

Through structured workflows, integrated tools, and a strong command of its features, Cursor doesn't just make you faster—it makes you a better developer. It helps you prioritize clarity, consistency, and quality over speed, enabling a higher standard of craftsmanship in your coding output.

Appendix

Glossary of AI and IDE Terms

AI (Artificial Intelligence): The simulation of human intelligence processes by machines, especially computer systems, enabling them to learn, reason, and self-correct.

IDE (Integrated Development Environment): A software suite that consolidates the basic tools developers need to write and test software, such as a code editor, debugger, and build automation tools.

Cursor AI: An AI-powered IDE that integrates advanced coding assistance, intelligent suggestions, and real-time debugging tools using large language models.

LLM (Large Language Model): A type of AI model trained on vast datasets to understand and generate human-like text, often used in AI coding assistants.

Prompt Engineering: The practice of designing inputs (prompts) to effectively guide the output of an AI model.

Refactoring: The process of restructuring existing computer code without changing its external behavior, typically to improve readability, maintainability, or performance.

CI/CD (Continuous Integration/Continuous Deployment): A set of practices that allow development teams to deliver code changes more frequently and reliably.

PR (Pull Request): A method of submitting contributions to a software project, often reviewed and discussed before merging into the main codebase.

Sample Configurations

Personal AI Configuration Example:

```
{ "verbosity": "concise",
  "tone": "neutral",
  "codeStyle": "camelCase",
  "languagePreference": "JavaScript",
  "assistantName": "CodeBuddy"}
```

Team-Wide Configuration Example:

```
{"promptTemplates": ["Write a unit test for this function", "Refactor this code for readability"],
```

```
"sharedSnippets":        ["apiCallTemplate",
"errorHandler"],
  "lintingRules": "standard",
  "integration": {"git": true, "ci": true}}
```

Resource Links: Updates, Plugins, Communities

- **Official Cursor AI Website:**
  https://www.cursor.so
- **GitHub Plugin Repositories:**
  https://github.com/cursor-so
- **Community Forum:**
  https://community.cursor.so
- **Updates and Roadmap:**
  https://updates.cursor.so
- **Cursor Discord Channel:**
  https://discord.gg/cursor

Troubleshooting Guide and FAQs

Cursor AI won't start:

- Ensure system meets minimum requirements.
- Try restarting the application or reinstalling it.
- Check for updates from the official website.

AI is generating incorrect or irrelevant suggestions:

- Adjust the prompt or verbosity settings.
- Ensure that the context is clear in the code block.

Cursor is not integrating with Git:

- Verify Git is installed and accessible via terminal.

- Check your repository settings and authentication keys.

Latency or slow performance:

- Switch from cloud-based AI to local model if supported.
- Close unused workspaces or tabs.
- Optimize your system's resources and ensure a stable internet connection.

AI-generated code has licensing concerns:

- Always review AI output.
- Use open-source compliant configurations.
- Refer to the Cursor license guidelines for best practices.

Cursor plugin isn't working:

- Confirm compatibility with your version.
- Visit the plugin's GitHub page for instructions and updates.

This appendix provides quick access to critical terms, resources, and solutions, helping you make the most of Cursor AI in your development workflow.

www.ingramcontent.com/pod-product-compliance
Lightning Source LLC
LaVergne TN
LVHW022343060326
832902LV00022B/4206